VOLTAIRE

Champion of the French Enlightenment

PHILOSOPHERS OF
THE ENLIGHTENMENT ™

VOLTAIRE
Champion of the French Enlightenment

Jason Porterfield

The Rosen Publishing Group, Inc., New York

Published in 2006 by The Rosen Publishing Group, Inc.
29 East 21st Street, New York, NY 10010

First Edition

Library of Congress Cataloging-in-Publication Data

Porterfield, Jason.
Voltaire: champion of the French enlightenment / by Jason Porterfield.—1st ed.
   p. cm.—(Philosophers of the Enlightenment)
Includes bibliographical references and index.
ISBN 1-4042-0423-7 (library binding: alk. paper)
1. Voltaire, 1694–1778.
I. Title. II. Series.
B2177.P67 2005
194—dc22

2004030624

Manufactured in Malaysia

On the cover: A 1736 portrait of Voltaire (foreground); a painting depicting a banquet at Ferney (background), Voltaire's Genevan estate from 1758 till the end of his life.

CONTENTS

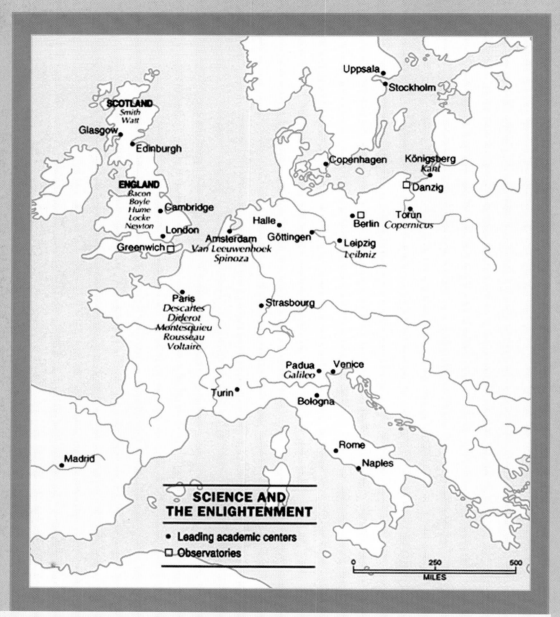

SCIENCE AND THE ENLIGHTENMENT

- • Leading academic centers
- ☐ Observatories

Uppsala
Stockholm
SCOTLAND
Smith
Watt
Glasgow
Edinburgh
Copenhagen
Königsberg
Kant
ENGLAND
Bacon
Boyle
Hume
Locke
Newton
Cambridge
London
Halle
Berlin
Danzig
Toruń
Copernicus
Amsterdam
Göttingen
Leipzig
Leibniz
Greenwich
Van Leeuwenhoek
Spinoza
Paris
Descartes
Diderot
Montesquieu
Rousseau
Voltaire
Strasbourg
Padua
Galileo
Venice
Turin
Bologna
Rome
Naples
Madrid

0   250   500
MILES

This map of western Europe shows the leading academic and scientific centers during the Enlightenment. It also lists many of the influential scientists and philosophers of the era. Although many historians place the Enlightenment in eighteenth-century France, the revolutionary outlook was really the product of the exchange of ideas across western Europe and spanned two centuries.

INTRODUCTION

On March 30, 1778, the great French writer Voltaire attended a performance of his newest play, *Irène*, with his niece Madame Marie Louise Denis at the famous Comédie Française in Paris. The theater was packed, and when he arrived, he was escorted to a special box seat and crowned with a wreath. As the play ended, the stage curtain rose one last time to reveal a marble bust of Voltaire. As verses were read in his honor, each member of the cast placed a wreath on the bust. Voltaire was delighted by this moving gesture, unparalleled in the history of French theater. The cast had paid tribute to the greatest living writer in all of France.

It was a momentous occasion in France's cultural world and in Voltaire's own life. He had just returned to

This eighteenth-century engraving depicts the "coronation" of Voltaire during the showing of his last play, *Irène*, at the Comédie Française in 1778. The scene is one of triumph for the philosopher, who had only recently returned to Paris from exile.

Paris after twenty-eight years in exile. More than 300 people visited him upon his arrival. Among them were many old friends, as well as new ones, such as Benjamin Franklin, the ambassador to France from the newly formed United States of America.

Voltaire deserved the attention. During his lifetime, he had established himself as a central figure in the Enlightenment, an era that lasted for much of the seventeenth century up until the American Revolution (1775–1783). The Enlightenment was

Here, Voltaire is captured in a confident—even arrogant—pose by his desk. Like the other Enlightenment philosophers, he challenged the established order with self-assurance, and, like many of his peers, he suffered the censure of his nation's religious and political leaders.

shaped by a number of writers, philosophers, scientists, and politicians who worked to use science, reason, and respect for humanity to change the world for the better. They saw themselves emerging to lead humanity away from centuries of darkness and superstition into the light of reason.

Voltaire was a key figure in advancing Enlightenment ideals. His poetry, dramas, historical and philosophical works, and his fiction all contributed to shape the world we live in today. His battles with religious and political authorities in France helped make people aware that they could make a difference by speaking out against injustice and intolerance. He endured imprisonment, exile, and persecution for his activities but continued his work with the phrase *écrasez l'infâme* ("crush the infamous") on his lips. Today he is remembered for those struggles as well as his groundbreaking writings.

FRANCE DURING THE TIME OF VOLTAIRE

CHAPTER 1

At the time of Voltaire's birth in 1694, France was one of the richest and most powerful nations in the world. Yet many of the kingdom's subjects lived in miserable poverty while the nobility enjoyed lives of privilege. The French monarchs had increased their power dramatically during the past century. The wealth and influence of the Catholic Church had also increased. While the church and the crown grew more powerful, many members of the lower classes suffered.

THE RULERS OF FRANCE

The seventeenth century was a period of change and turmoil in France. During the late sixteenth century, a long and bloody clash between Protestants

France's King Henry IV's short reign was marked by economic prosperity and progressive social changes for the lower class. Voltaire praised King Henry in his epic poem, "La Henriade," holding up the monarch as a model of a great leader.

and Catholics called the Wars of Religion bankrupted the kingdom and disrupted life across France. Many members of the lower classes suffered greatly.

Under the rule of King Henry IV (reigned 1589–1610), France underwent a period of economic recovery and growth. Henry IV restored the royal finances, improved roads, and built canals. He brought in artisans from other parts of Europe to start new industries. He even introduced the cultivation of silk worms so that France's silk industry would have its own domestic supply. More important, he reduced the misery of the lower classes by forbidding creditors from seizing livestock or tools, canceling overdue property tax debts, and selling off public lands for below market value.

Henry IV left a booming economy for his successor, Louis XIII (r. 1610–1643). The new king and his able minister, the Cardinal Armand-Jean du Plessis de Richelieu, greatly reduced the power of the French nobility. They split the country into thirty administrative districts, each governed by a royal minister loyal to the crown. Richelieu increased France's stature in the world by founding the French navy and encouraging foreign trade and colonial expansion.

Richelieu's policies proved expensive. Growing inflation and high taxes once again made life difficult for the poor. Additionally, the Thirty Years' War threatened to engulf France. The war, which began in 1618 as a German civil war, spread across Europe as various allied nations became involved. Richelieu brought France into the war in 1635. When the war ended in 1648, France had increased its territories and emerged as a great power.

While France asserted itself internationally, it suffered internally. The war took a great toll on the countryside, bringing even worse living conditions to the lower classes. No fewer than five peasant uprisings were suppressed during the reign of Louis XIII.

THE SUN KING'S RISE

Louis XIII died in 1643, five years before the war ended. The four-year-old Louis XIV was crowned

Louis XIV of France (shown here about to strike the ball at the billiard table) is one of history's best examples of an absolute monarch. During his reign, political power in France was concentrated in his hands and in those of a few trusted advisers. He was demonstrably opulent, and he used the wealth of the crown to both coax and control his noblemen. His extravagance and his wars to dominate the world left France bankrupt.

king of France in 1643. He did not take power until his regent and prime minister, the Cardinal Mazarin, died in 1661.

The Sun King, as Louis XIV came to be called, broke from French political tradition and refused to name another prime minister. Instead, he chose to rule on his own. France fought four wars during his reign, increasing its power and territory after each conflict. When Louis XIV died in 1715, France had few international rivals.

The Sun King worked to further centralize royal authority. He ordered the nobility to serve as members of his court, stripping them of their power as regional officials. He had a lavish palace built just outside of Paris at Versailles and made it his seat of command. By having the nobility serve him there, he prevented them from increasing their own strength in their hometowns. In this way, Louis XIV ruled as an absolute monarch, meaning that all of the political power of France rested in his hands.

France's treasury stood near bankruptcy when Louis XIV took over. His expensive wars and lifestyle further drained the economy. Corruption was widespread throughout the financial bureaucracy. Nobles and members of the clergy were exempt from taxation. The burden of paying France's debts was placed on the peasantry and the emerging bourgeoisie, or middle class.

The arts flourished during Louis XIV's reign. His palace at Versailles remains a beautiful testament to French architecture and sculpture, while the palace gardens elevated landscaping to a fine art.

Louis loved art in many forms. He encouraged the French Academy, an organization of writers founded by Richelieu in 1635, to discuss literary matters. He supported the Academy of Painting and

Sculpture, founded in 1648, and brought about the establishment of the Academy of Architecture in 1675. These groups were meant to raise the public's taste in their respective fields. Louis XIV also offered pensions to writers he respected, supported the theater, and appointed an official to oversee the development of French music.

THE CATHOLIC CHURCH

By the end of the seventeenth century, the Roman Catholic Church was the most powerful institution in France apart from the monarchy itself. The church possessed about one-fifth of France's wealth, yet it paid no taxes. Many clergymen were corrupt. They took advantage of the superstitious peasantry to increase their wealth and power. Religious persecution was common. Those who questioned Catholic teachings or spoke against the church were often punished, sometimes horribly. During the course of his life, Voltaire frequently found himself facing persecution from religious officials. In his later years, he would make a name for himself by standing up for others facing persecution.

The Catholic Church had absolute sway over the spiritual lives of French subjects. The Jesuits were the dominant sect. They were largely dedicated to education and reform. The Jesuits were particularly powerful because they served as confessors and advisers to French monarchs. Their loyalty to the pope and influence within the royal court gave the church considerable political influence.

PROTESTANTISM AND RELIGIOUS STRIFE

During the 1540s, a French Protestant named John Calvin founded a strict Protestant religious movement. Thousands of people among both the nobility and the lower classes converted to Calvinism. They called themselves Huguenots.

King Henry II viewed the Huguenots as a threat to royal authority and vowed to crush the sect. His efforts to wipe out Calvinism led to the Wars of Religion. These conflicts were marked by brutality on both sides. The violence culminated in 1572 with the Saint Bartholomew's Day Massacre, when a Catholic mob attacked and killed thousands of Huguenots.

An uneasy calm was restored when Henry IV issued the Edict of Nantes in 1598. The document offered French Huguenots freedom to worship in specified towns and castles and allowed them to hold public office. It marked the first time that a European leader offered his or her subjects freedom

The Saint Bartholomew's Day Massacre is one of the most dreadful holocausts in history. Up to 100,000 Protestants were killed by mobs led by French soldiers and members of the Roman Catholic clergy. The massacre was ordered by Queen Catherine de' Médicis and continued long after she ordered it to stop. This drawing shows the queen viewing victims on a street in Paris.

of religion in any form. Many Catholics were upset by what they saw as a royal acceptance of heretical beliefs. In 1610, a religious fanatic assassinated Henry IV.

The Edict of Nantes remained in force until Louis XIV revoked it in 1685 by issuing the Edict of Fontainebleau. The new law denied Huguenots the right to worship publicly, closed their schools, called for the destruction of their churches, and ordered all Huguenot clergy out of the country.

DEISM

Deism flourished throughout Europe as an alternative to existing factions of Christianity during the seventeenth and eighteenth centuries. Deists believed they could discern the will of God through the use of reason. They also rejected organized religion. The movement encouraged rational criticisms of religion and discouraged fanaticism and intolerance toward other viewpoints. Many of the Enlightenment thinkers, including Voltaire and the English philosopher John Locke, were deists. In turn, they influenced others to take a rational approach to religion.

About 200,000 Huguenots left France soon afterward. Their departure dealt a severe blow to the country's already strained economy, as many Huguenots were skilled artisans who had been vital to France's economic welfare.

Around 1640, yet another religious sect emerged to threaten the power of the Catholic hierarchy. Jansenism was a very strict form of Catholicism based on the theories of Flemish theologian Cornelius Jansen. The sect was founded on the idea of predestination, the belief that God has already decided an individual's fate after death. Jansenists believed that people were born evil and remained that way unless they received divine help through the grace of God. They also believed that only a select number of people could get into heaven. In order to receive God's grace and increase their chances of entering heaven, Jansenists had to make very careful lifestyle choices, live simply, and stick to a strict schedule of prayer and meditation.

The Catholic Church opposed the Jansenists, though Jansenists viewed themselves as Catholics. The pope condemned a series of five propositions relating to predestination in 1653. Pressured by the church, Louis XIV committed himself to ridding France of Jansenists, and Jansenist teachings were condemned. In 1709, the king closed the Jansenist convent of Port-Royal-des-Champs. It was destroyed one year later. The movement thrived despite the loss of its headquarters and steadily grew in influence. By the 1760s, the Jansenists were powerful enough to force the Jesuits out of France.

A LIFE OF WIT AND DRAMA

Voltaire was born François-Marie Arouet into a middle-class Parisian family on November 21, 1694. His mother died when he was only seven, and the rest of his family expected the sickly child to follow. His health remained uncertain throughout his long life, and he fretted frequently about illness.

After his mother's death, his older sister, Marguerite-Catherine, cared for him until her marriage. His early education was directed by his godfather, the Abbé de Châteauneuf. His father, an ambitious and successful lawyer, sent him off to a fashionable Paris boarding school called Louis-le-grand in 1704. The school was run by Jesuit priests, who gave him an excellent background in early Greek and Latin drama. It was there that the young Arouet first displayed his wit and poetic ability.

Many of the ideas of the Enlightenment were proposed, discussed, and debated at social gatherings called salons. These events fostered networks of social and intellectual exchange that connected Paris to the rest of France.

Arouet knew from an early age that he wanted to write. Many of his Jesuit teachers praised his skill at writing verse. His father, however, viewed writing as a disreputable and unprofitable way of life. When Arouet finished his education at Louis-le-grand in 1711, his father immediately sent him off to study law with the hope of later buying him a political office.

Arouet had little interest in law and spent most of his time socializing with writers and philosophers. When he was seventeen years old, his godfather introduced him to the members of the Temple, a group of writers and intellectuals, who welcomed the teenager. Many of the literary stars of the day circulated within this learned crowd.

Other doors into Paris's intellectual world were unwittingly opened by Arouet's own parents. They had frequently hosted the groundbreaking French playwright Pierre Corneille until his death ten years before Arouet was born. The poet and critic Nicolas Boileau-Despréaux, known for his poetic satires, was another family friend whom Arouet warmly recalled. Louis de Plessis, the future Duke of Richelieu, was the son of a family friend and a descendant of Cardinal Richelieu's. He would remain one of Arouet's close friends. Charles Ferriol, the future Comte d'Argental, became another valuable lifelong friend.

Arouet became a desired guest in the fashionable homes and salons in Paris. His quick wit and light verse had made him widely known. His father, in an act of desperation, sent him out of Paris to get him away from his own fame. When Arouet went to Caen to study law, it was the first of a series of exiles he would pass in his lifetime. He did little studying and soon found himself back in Paris.

THE REGENCY OF PHILIPPE II

Louis XIV died in 1715, just as Arouet was making a name for himself as a wit and poet. He was succeeded by his five-year-old great-grandson, Louis XV. Until the new king came of age, France was ruled by his uncle and regent, Philippe II, Duke of Orléans. Philippe was not as strong a leader as Louis XIV had

Philippe II, Duke of Orléans, was regent of France between 1715 and 1723, when he died. He was not a strong leader, but many of his policies were welcomed by the major intellectual figures of his time. He was against censorship, and he ordered the reprinting of books banned by his predecessor. He also opened the royal library to the public.

been, and he inherited a kingdom that was clearly on the decline. However, the regent was an intelligent man who attempted to reverse some of Louis XIV's failed or oppressive policies. Philippe became an even greater patron of the arts than the Sun King had been. He promoted education, allowed books that had been banned by Louis XIV to be printed, and surrounded himself with writers and artists.

Philippe was a controversial figure in Paris. In his hands, the economy continued to decline. Rumors about his immoral lifestyle spread freely. Even worse in the eyes of the Catholic Church, Philippe was an atheist who scarcely bothered to hide his beliefs.

Arouet's sharp wit and popularity had upset some among Paris's cultural elite, and it seemed that the defiant young poet was headed for a fall. In 1717, certain verses written in his style circulated throughout the city. They implied that the regent was having an affair with his own daughter. Arouet was arrested, though he denied writing the verses. He was sent to the Bastille, the notorious prison where political prisoners were sometimes held without charges until they were forgotten.

He remained there for eleven months. He was treated well, given a light, airy cell, and was allowed many visitors. Yet the experience changed him forever. Arouet entered the prison a composer of light, meaningless verse. By the time of his release, he had become a serious writer, determined to end the sort of social injustices that had led to his own imprisonment. To signify this change, the young writer began signing his name as "Voltaire." Voltaire never explained how he settled on his new name. However, some literary scholars speculate that it is a shortened version of his childhood nickname "le petit volontaire," which means "little willful one."

Voltaire emerged from the Bastille in April 1718 and immediately went into forced exile in the French countryside. There, he began writing furiously, polishing a play he had been working on since he was eighteen. By fall, he had finished writing *Oedipe*, though he initially had trouble finding actors to fill the roles. He later wrote to his friend and former teacher Charles Porée, "I had much difficulty in getting the Parisian actors to consent to perform even the choruses which appear three or four times in the play. I had even more to get accepted a tragedy almost without love."

The play premiered on November 18, 1718, and became a huge success. It ran for forty-five nights before closing. After the play's run, Voltaire's name was known across France. Copies of the play were immediately printed and read throughout Paris. The young writer made a small fortune out of the play's popularity.

Oedipe won praise from critics and dramatists alike. The regent also enjoyed the drama, though he was the target of some of its satire. Voltaire became a favorite of the royal court. Voltaire even sent a copy of the play to King George I of England, who sent him a gold medal and a watch in return. Voltaire was thrilled by all of the attention.

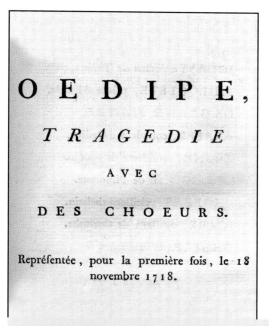

OEDIPE,

TRAGEDIE

AVEC

DES CHOEURS.

Repréfentée, pour la première fois, le 18 novembre 1718.

This is the title page of Voltaire's *Oedipe*. The note at the bottom of the page reads, "Performed, for the first time, November 18, 1718." In addition to being a theatrical success, *Oedipe* turned a handsome profit in print form.

Voltaire's ailing father attended a performance. He forgave Voltaire for going against his wishes after seeing *Oedipe*'s success for himself. When he died in 1722, he left Voltaire a third of his fortune.

EXILE TO ENGLAND

Voltaire spent the next few years writing, increasing his wealth, and enjoying his fame. The regent died

This nineteenth-century painting shows Voltaire while he was imprisoned in the Bastille. Although embittered by his imprisonment, the young writer spent his time there productively, working on a number of projects. His incarceration certainly must have influenced his opposition to religious and political persecution.

in 1724, leaving France in the hands of the insecure Louis XV. Despite having Voltaire imprisoned in the Bastille, Philippe had been a valuable ally. The young king was not as tolerant. He bowed to the pressure of the Catholic Church and ordered Voltaire's epic poem "La Henriade" condemned. Voltaire was upset by this royal reaction but encouraged copies be secretly circulated.

Voltaire had ridden a great wave of public success since *Oedipe* premiered, but his life soon took an ugly turn. He and the Chevalier de Rohan-Chabot engaged in a public quarrel in late 1725. A few weeks after they began exchanging insults, four thugs hired by the chevalier beat Voltaire as Rohan-Chabot looked on. The furious writer attempted to bring legal action against Rohan-Chabot, but the difference in their social standing—the chevalier was a nobleman while Voltaire was a member of the middle class—made it almost impossible for Voltaire to fight back without support from other noblemen. None of his powerful friends came to his aid.

Voltaire began taking fencing lessons, hoping to challenge the chevalier to a duel. The chevalier retaliated by having Voltaire arrested and taken to the Bastille. Furious at the injustice of sitting in a cell while the man who had ordered him beaten went free, Voltaire offered a proposition: if released from prison, he would immediately leave France. The authorities accepted, and Voltaire was released on April 29, 1726, twenty-one days after his arrest. He boarded a ship for England four days later, beginning an exile that lasted for three years.

Voltaire plunged into English society with relish. He had long viewed England as a tolerant paradise, where religious authorities did not influence the government and opposing views were not suppressed. Within months, he mastered the English language. He began making friends with many of England's greatest writers, including Alexander Pope and Jonathan Swift. He visited friends regularly and began selling his English translation of "La Henriade."

Voltaire voraciously read the works of English writers and investigated the ideas of English thinkers. He was particularly attracted to the political philosophy of John Locke. Locke had argued against the divine right of kings to rule, contending that state sovereignty belonged to the people. Locke had also stated that governments should be responsible for protecting the rights of the people and that church and state should be separated. Voltaire later drew on many of these ideas in his own writings. His studies of Shakespeare's dramas and the science of Sir Isaac Newton also laid the foundation for later works.

RETURN TO FRANCE

Voltaire returned to France in 1729 with several projects in progress. During his years in England, he had increased both his knowledge and his fortune. Several of his plays appeared shortly after his return, including *Brutus* in 1730 and *Zaïre* in 1732. Both opened successfully.

John Locke was one of the most influential writers in England during the late seventeenth century. Many of the later Enlightenment thinkers drew on and expanded upon his philosophy surrounding human rights.

During Voltaire's lifetime, anything a writer wanted to publish officially had to meet the approval of a government censor. Voltaire soon found himself in trouble after publishing several works without official permission, including a satirical essay called "The Temple of Taste" ("Le Temple du Goût") in 1733. One of Voltaire's most famous works, *Philosophical Letters, or Letters Concerning the English Nation* (*Lettres Philosophiques, ou Lettres sur les Anglais*), appeared without official permission in

Voltaire wrote many of his important works at the Château de Cirey (shown here in this eighteenth-century engraving) in Haute marne, France. He lived there with his lover, Emilie du Châtelet, with whom he worked on many scientific projects.

1734. This work upset the royal court and the religious hierarchy so much that Voltaire once again had to flee Paris.

Voltaire retreated to the remote Château de Cirey—roughly 155 miles (250 kilometers) from Paris—and home to his lover Emilie du Châtelet. Voltaire remained there for fifteen years, writing and conducting scientific experiments with Emilie. Though far from Paris, they received many guests and Voltaire's fame spread.

Voltaire found it easy to work in the countryside. During this period, he began a long correspondence with Crown Prince Frederick of Prussia. He also completed his most famous scientific work, *Elements of the Philosophy of Newton* (*Éléments de la Philosophie de Newton*, 1736). His philosophical description of the human condition, *Discourse on Man* (*Discours sur l'Homme*), appeared in 1738. A short work on the life of Louis XIV, *Essay on the Century of Louis XIV* (*Essai sur le Siècle de Louis XIV*), was published in 1739. He later expanded this short volume into *The Century of Louis XIV* (*Le Siècle de Louis XIV*) in 1751. He also produced several plays during this time, including *Alzire* (1736), *Mahomet* (1742), *Mérope* (1743), and *Sémiramis* (1748).

Though he was far from Paris, both the Crown and the academic world honored him during this period. In 1745, he was appointed royal historiographer. The king made him a gentleman of the king's bedchamber the next year, granting him official access to all parts of the palace. That same year, his peers elected him as a member of the French Academy, an honor he had dreamed about for years. Sadly, Emilie died in 1749, bringing an end to the most settled and peaceful period of Voltaire's life.

THE WANDERING EXILE

CHAPTER 3

Voltaire left Cirey upon Emilie du Châtelet's death. He returned to Paris for a time but was soon pressured to leave after criticizing King Louis XV. Voltaire had long put off an invitation to live in Berlin extended by his friend Prince Frederick, now King Frederick II of Prussia (also known as Frederick the Great). He finally accepted in 1750.

Voltaire's stay in Berlin did not go well. King Frederick proved to be a vain and demanding host, far different from the sensitive philosopher-king Voltaire had expected. Frederick prided himself on collecting great minds for his court and viewed his acquisition of Voltaire as his crowning achievement.

Voltaire soon made his life in Berlin worse by denouncing and insulting other members of Frederick's

This undated illustration by Jules Girardet shows Voltaire being taken into custody in Prussia by order of his old friend King Frederick II. Almost everywhere that Voltaire went, his words sparked controversy that often landed him in a lot of trouble.

intellectual circle. The scientist Pierre de Maupertuis was the leader of this group, and he had a low opinion of Voltaire. The feeling was mutual. In 1752, Voltaire published a satire of Maupertuis's work entitled *Diatribe of Doctor Akakia* (*Diatribe du Docteur Akakia*). Frederick condemned *Diatribe* and threatened to have Voltaire arrested. By this time, Voltaire was eager to leave, but the king was proud of having lured Europe's most renowned writer to his court and had no intention of letting him go. Voltaire eventually had to sneak out of Berlin in 1753.

GENEVA

Voltaire next headed to Geneva in present-day Switzerland. At that time, Geneva was an independent republic famous for its tolerance. The city was also dominated by Calvinists, a sect that Voltaire considered more politically open-minded than the Catholic hierarchy in France. In 1754, he settled down just outside the city with his niece Madame Marie Louise Denis.

The city welcomed them with open arms but soon soured on Voltaire, who violated its strict laws by building a theater and giving performances. More bad feeling was generated after he was accused of contributing to an unflattering article about Geneva, written for Denis Diderot and Jean Le Rond d'Alembert's groundbreaking *Encyclopedia, or Reasoned Dictionary of the Sciences, Arts, and Trades* (*Encyclopédie ou Dictionnaire Raisonné des Sciences, des Arts et des Metiers*). Because Voltaire had written a number of articles for the work and was close to both men, the charge was likely true. The incident alienated him from the city and its people. Despite a rocky relationship with Geneva's government, Voltaire remained busy during his stay there, continually writing plays and working on articles for Diderot's *Encyclopedia*.

During his stay in Geneva, a massive earthquake destroyed the Portuguese city of Lisbon, killing 90,000 people. Voltaire commemorated the tragedy in "Poem on the Lisbon Disaster" ("Poème sur le Désastre de Lisbonne") in 1755. The Lisbon earthquake ultimately impacted much of his later work.

FERNEY

Voltaire soon tired of battling Geneva's authorities. In 1758, he purchased an estate called Ferney in Geneva's countryside, near the border with France. As a safety precaution, he also bought a house just within the French border at a place called Tourney. The properties were only a few miles apart, which made it easy for Voltaire to escape to one country if he faced persecution in the other. He made Ferney his home until almost the end of his life.

Voltaire worked strenuously to improve his estate. He made extensive repairs to the house and gardens. When he saw that most of the Ferney's peasants lived in miserable hovels, he had new houses built for them. He further improved their lives by adding a stocking factory and a watch works. He also renovated the estate's chapel, having the words *Deo erexit Voltaire* ("Voltaire erected this to God") carved into the facade. At Voltaire's request,

This engraving shows Voltaire's famous country estate in Ferney, Geneva. Here, Voltaire held court, welcoming visitors from all walks of life, and wrote some of his most important works. It is during his time at Ferney that he was most engaged in social activism, particularly his crusades against religious intolerance.

the pope sent him a holy relic to commemorate the occasion. Nevertheless, Voltaire used the chapel to preach deist sermons to a captive audience of his tenants and employees.

Ferney soon became a magnet for writers, philosophers, and other famous or curious visitors. Voltaire threw his doors open to all guests, no matter how busy he was or how ill he felt. He generously helped those who came to him in need, and Ferney filled with relatives and friends who had nowhere else to go.

One of the greatest examples of Voltaire's generosity came about in 1760, when he learned that Marie Corneille, a young relative of the playwright Pierre Corneille, was living in poverty. Voltaire immediately invited the girl to live at Ferney. When she arrived, Voltaire adopted her. He and Madame Denis saw to her education, and the old philosopher doted over her as though she were his own daughter.

Voltaire also began working on a standard edition of Corneille's works, complete with a detailed commentary. The finished product appeared in 1766 in twelve volumes. Voltaire sold copies all over Europe and to twenty-one royal houses through his many correspondents. As he wrote to his friend Philip, fourth Earl of Chesterfield, "I have as a scribbler, made a pretty curious commentary on many tragedies of Corneille. [It] is my duty since the [granddaughter] of Corneille is in my house. If there was a [granddaughter] of Shakespeare, I would subscribe for her." The book generated a small fortune, all of which became Marie Corneille's.

Voltaire began taking part in public controversies, working on behalf of people whom he felt had been wronged by the French government or the Catholic Church. He put his writing skills, vast network of friends, and boundless energy to work as a crusader against injustice. His most famous case

Despite Voltaire's vigilant efforts in his defense, Jean Calas, a French Protestant cloth merchant, was tortured and executed on charges that he had murdered his son. Here, Calas is shown being broken on the wheel, before he was strangled and burned. This type of punishment was common in eighteenth-century France, especially for Protestant convicts.

was that of the Calas family, Huguenots who had been wrongly accused and convicted of murdering one of their children in 1762. Though the father was executed, Voltaire used his influence, energy, and writing skills to have the convictions reversed and the family's reputation restored. Other similar incidents followed as Voltaire discovered the power of public opinion and learned how to use it.

Voltaire waited until after the family's acquittal before publishing one of his most moving pleas for

DIDEROT'S *ENCYCLOPEDIA*

In 1747, an obscure playwright, critic, and philosopher named Denis Diderot began working on a French translation of Ephraim Chambers's *Cyclopaedia*, a two-volume collection of knowledge written in England in 1728. With the help of the mathematician Jean Le Rond d'Alembert, Diderot began converting the translation into a massive philosophical work. He enlisted some of the greatest minds of the era to help write articles, including Voltaire, Jean-Jacques Rousseau, and Charles-Louis Montesquieu. Diderot began printing the *Encyclopedia* in 1751. He often faced persecution for his work and was forced to secretly print the final seven volumes. The work was completed in 1765, but Diderot added to it until 1780. When finished, the *Encyclopedia* had become a thirty-five-volume weapon against superstition and the power of the Catholic Church and nobility.

Denis Diderot, a writer and philosopher, was the editor of the Encyclopedia, *perhaps the single most important publication of the Enlightenment.*

reason, his *Treatise on Toleration* in 1764. The work begins by detailing Jean Calas' unjust torture and execution. From there, it examines cruelties and intolerance throughout history. He concludes that humanity's intolerance and mistakes are only seen as such if they disturb society, which usually only happens when these crimes are due to fanaticism. Voltaire calls for an end to fanatical behavior and for people to view each other as reasonable, feeling beings. People should end all fanaticism in order to merit tolerance:

> The fewer dogmas, the fewer disputes; the fewer disputes, the fewer miseries: if this is not true, then I'm wrong. Religion was instituted to make us happy in this life and in the other. What must we do to be happy in the life to come? Be just.

Voltaire published his most famous work, the short novel *Candide*, soon after moving to Ferney in 1758. Another of his landmark works, the *Philosophical Dictionary* (*Dictionnaire Philosophique*), appeared in 1764. The work contained all of the articles Voltaire had contributed to his friend Diderot's *Encyclopedia*. His writings during this period reflected the themes that directed his actions throughout his long life. Through his words, Voltaire tried to convince his country to establish religious tolerance, respect individual rights, and put an end to torture and unjust punishments. Through his efforts to encourage people to think for themselves, he undermined the absolute control that the king and the Catholic Church exercised over France. His astute use of public opinion to direct social outrage at abuses of power helped set the French Revolution in motion.

A TRIUMPHANT RETURN

Louis XV died in 1774. To the end, he had little regard for Voltaire. He was succeeded by Louis XVI, who took a more tolerant view on Europe's most renowned writer. Voltaire was optimistic about this new ruler and began considering leaving Ferney.

Voltaire made his famous return to Paris four years later. He spent the first few months of 1778 bustling about Paris, visiting old friends, and working with the French Academy to begin a historical dictionary of the French language. All of this activity proved too much for his fragile health. Voltaire died in Paris on May 26, 1778.

VOLTAIRE'S DRAMA AND POETRY

CHAPTER 4

Voltaire was known chiefly as a poet and a dramatist during his lifetime. Between fifty and sixty plays are attributed to him, some existing only as fragments. Most of his plays are tragedies, though even these contain elements of satirical humor. Most were well received by the theatergoing public, and they were popular and widely performed during Voltaire's day. Few of his dramas are still performed today, however.

The majority of his poems are little more than light fragments or witty epigrams. He produced very few significant poems, but those that did appear were widely read. Some, such as "La Henriade," are considered French classics.

This carving shows Marie-Françoise Trader, a leading tragic actress of the eighteenth century, playing the role of Jocasta in Voltaire's *Oedipe*. Over time, Voltaire became quite popular among Paris's actors. In addition to writing some of the best known works of his time, he treated and paid his cast members well.

OEDIPE

The tragedy *Oedipe* (1718) was Voltaire's first drama, completed and produced shortly after the end of his first stay in the Bastille. Voltaire had begun working on a draft as early as 1716, when he was still introducing himself into the literary world at the Temple. He read it out loud to his friends in the Temple and in drawing rooms all over France before finally having it produced.

Oedipe is based on the ancient Greek drama *Oedipus Tyrannus* by Sophocles. Voltaire's interpretation builds upon an earlier French version by Corneille. The play is about a man who unwittingly kills his real father, marries his mother, and becomes a king. These events touch off a series of plagues within the city he rules. The plagues stop when the truth of the situation is revealed, but it is too late for the main characters. The queen commits suicide, and Oedipus blinds himself for his crimes.

Reinterpreting the works of two great masters of theater was a very bold step. The public would judge it against the works of Sophocles and Corneille. Voltaire's play had thirty almost-consecutive performances, a feat unmatched by any other drama performed in France during the eighteenth century. *Oedipe*'s success owed a great deal to a growing distrust within French society of the Catholic Church and the government. The play openly ridiculed the religious hierarchy. At one point, Oedipus's mother, Jocasta, announces, "Our priests are not what an idle populace imagines, their knowledge is merely our credulity." Despite the anti-authoritarian tone of lines such as "Kings cannot read men's hearts; their blows often fall on the inno-cent," the regent Philippe had the play performed at the royal court.

MARIAMNE AND BRUTUS

Voltaire's experimental play *Mariamne* appeared in 1724. It broke theater tradition by ending with the title character's onstage suicide. During that era, death only took place offstage. The play was a fail-ure. It was shown only once before Voltaire stopped the production and began revising it. The new version, called *Herod and Mariamne* (*Hérode et Mariamne*), opened the next year without the onstage death and was a great success.

Brutus (1730) was the first truly noteworthy play Voltaire produced after his return from England in 1729. The title refers to a Roman politician named Lucius Junius Brutus. Conspirators manipulate Brutus throughout the play in an attempt to bring

democratic Rome under the rule of the tyrant Tarquin. The Roman senate ultimately forces him to sentence his own son for acting as a spy. Brutus sentences his son to death rather than corruptly use his political power to save him. Rather, Brutus asks that his colleagues follow his example in ruling for the good of the people. *Brutus* incorporates some of Voltaire's most radical ideas about government, reflecting Voltaire's smoldering resentment over his imprisonment and exile. The play openly states that the government should exist to represent the needs of the people rather than the desires of the powerful.

ZAÏRE AND *ALZIRE*

Voltaire wrote one of his greatest tragedies, *Zaïre*, during the summer of 1732. *Zaïre* was completed in just three weeks and opened on August 13, 1732. It became an immediate success and was performed thirty-one times that year.

This portrait of Voltaire shows the philosopher at work in his study—most likely at Ferney—around 1766. By this time, Voltaire was sufficiently wealthy enough to be considered a country gentleman. He became known as the squire of Ferney all across Europe. Ferney itself came to be viewed as the continent's intellectual capital.

This illustration from the 1785 complete edition of *L'Imprimerie de la Société Litteraire-Typographique* (The Printed Works of the Literary-Typographic Society), shows a scene from a performance of Voltaire's *Zaïre*.

Zaïre is one of several Christian slaves in the service of Orosmane, the Muslim sultan of Jerusalem. The sultan loves and intends to marry Zaïre, who loves him in return. Their plans to marry are wrecked by Nérestan, a Christian who left Jerusalem to buy the freedom of the sultan's slaves. When Nérestan returns, Orosmane declares that he will free all the slaves except Zaïre.

Meanwhile, Orosmane becomes jealous while watching Zaïre and Nérestan interact, not knowing that they are really brother and sister. Nérestan tells Zaïre of their father's dying wish that she return to Christianity, and she promises to postpone her marriage to Orosmane until after she sees a priest. Orosmane's suspicions deepen when he learns of the delay, and he kills Zaïre in a rage. When he shows her body to Nérestan, he realizes that they are brother and sister and kills himself out of grief.

In this play, Voltaire uses a love story as the setting for a discussion of religion. The play subtly attacks the power wielded by the church hierarchy over ordinary people and the Jansenist idea of grace. He illustrates how religious faith ultimately has no power over passion. The love between Orosmane and Zaïre shows that one's religious faith is determined by the place of one's birth more than any other factor. As Zaïre states in the first act of the play, "The care taken of our childhood forms our feelings, our habits, our belief. By the Ganges I would have been a slave of the false gods, a Christian in Paris, a Muslim here." Their respective faiths do not come between them until her family starts meddling.

The tragedy *Alzire* (1736) appeared four years later. This play is the earliest surviving French drama set in the Americas. It tells the story of Gusman, a Spaniard who has been ordered to govern Peru. His subjects are Native Americans who have converted to Christianity, and he is told to rule them with Christian moderation. Gusman begins his task in this spirit but soon falls in love with the princess Alzire. Frustrated when Alzire fails to return his love, he grows increasingly cruel.

Alzire's father encourages her to marry Gusman to appease the Spanish invaders, and she reluctantly obeys. Her true love, the unconverted king Zamore, attacks the city and fatally wounds Gusman. Zamore is arrested and sentenced to death along with Alzire, who helped the attackers. Gusman offers to pardon Zamore if he becomes a Christian, but the proud king refuses. Gusman pardons both of them before dying, showing them the merits of Christian charity.

VOLTAIRE'S LATER PLAYS

Mérope appeared in 1743 and told the same basic story as Voltaire's earlier play *Mahomet* (1742). Both plays feature powerful religious or political leaders who are gradually corrupted by power. In the case of *Mahomet*, the main character turns the peaceful doctrines of his faith into an excuse to conquer. The main character in *Mérope* is the tyrant Polyphonte,

This is an illustration from "La Henriade." It shows subjects bowing respectively as King Henry IV enters a street in Paris on horseback. Even the heavenly creatures (holding a lantern and an olive branch) appear to be saluting the king, reflecting Voltaire's view that Henry IV was an enlightened monarch.

Les remparts ébranlés s'entr'ouvrent à fa voix.

Il entre au nom du Dieu qui fait régner les Rois.

who uses the fear and fanaticism of his subjects to remain in power.

Voltaire had several dramatic successes after producing *Mérope*, though few were of the same quality. *Sémiramis* appeared in 1748, telling the story of a Babylonian queen. His comedy *Nanine* appeared the same year. *Nanine* was one of the few comedies Voltaire ever produced and was a moderate success. *Tancrède*, produced in 1760, closely follows the same themes as *Zaïre*. With *Tancrède*, the tale of corrupt power and thwarted love takes place in medieval France, a time of glorified chivalry. Voltaire closed his career as a writer with the tragedy *Irène* in 1778.

VOLTAIRE THE POET

Voltaire first made a name for himself in literary circles as a writer of light verse. During his lifetime, he wrote volumes of such poems. As a poet, he is best remembered as the writer of "La Henriade," the first true epic poem in the history of French literature. Voltaire began writing the poem in 1717, while imprisoned in the Bastille. He spent several years working on it before having an early draft secretly printed in 1723.

"La Henriade" relates the story of King Henry IV of France, emphasizing the wrongs committed in the name of religion throughout history. Voltaire took care to speak in defense of non-Christians, writing that:

> God does not punish them for having closed their eyes to the knowledge which he himself placed so far from them; he does not judge them like an unjust master because of the Christian laws they had no means of knowing, because of the insensate zeal of their sacred rage, but by the simple law which appeals to all hearts.

Copies smuggled into Paris sold well despite official condemnation from the Catholic Church. Voltaire made a fortune with the proceeds from an English translation printed in 1728. He was finally allowed to officially publish "La Henriade" in France in 1730. It received wide acclaim.

Most of Voltaire's significant poems criticize religion, but none more so than "Epistle to Uranis" ("Epître à Uranie," 1732). Voltaire first composed it in 1722, during a trip to Geneva, where he saw people of many different faiths living together in harmony. The poem was written as a response to the wavering faith of his traveling companion, Madame de Rupelmonde.

In the poem, he questions how a just God could allow cruelty to survive on Earth. He ultimately declared that he could not be a Christian under such a god, and urged Madame de Rupelmonde to choose one way or another. The poem set Voltaire solidly against the intolerance and superstition that characterized the Catholic Church at the time. It also emphasized that just and virtuous people of any faith could find peace and joy in God through their actions. Those who professed their faith while acting contrary to God's teachings could never receive grace. The poem reads, in part:

> Ah! what matter indeed by what name he be implored? Every homage is received, but none does him honour. A god has no need of our assiduous attentions: if he can be offended, it is only by injustice; he judges by our virtues, and not by our sacrifices.

For years, he kept the poem under lock and key. When it finally began circulating in 1732, Voltaire denied authorship to avoid persecution.

He published an essay in verse form called "The Temple of Taste" in 1732. Voltaire used this satire to bemoan what he saw as a decline in the arts in France since the time of Louis XIV. "La Pucelle"

Much like the 2004 tsunami in southeastern Asia, the 1755 Lisbon earthquake was a major catastrophe that took a lot of lives and destroyed the properties and livelihood of the survivors. Many people, including Voltaire, questioned why a just God would allow such a tragedy to happen.

(1755) uses Voltaire's most devastating weapon, his wit, to criticize the church. "La Pucelle" is a bawdy retelling of the Joan of Arc legend. Voltaire describes many of Joan's adventures, questioning her visions from God, and mocking the church's faith in her purity of spirit.

Voltaire composed his most moving poem after the Lisbon earthquake of 1755. "Poem on the Lisbon Disaster" expresses Voltaire's grief that such a horrible event could occur. In it, he devotes many lines to his anger at the philosophy of optimism, developed by

OPTIMISM

The word "optimism" originally referred to a philosophy developed by a German thinker named Gottfried Leibniz. In 1710, he published a work explaining that suffering and evil are necessary elements of life. Without them, the world would seem diminished. Optimism fit in very well with the popular view of the time that this world was only one of an infinite number of possible worlds. Because God chose to create Earth as it is, it must be the best of all possible worlds. Therefore, all that happens on Earth must be for the greater good. Leibniz suggested that if we saw the world from God's perspective, we would conclude that everything took place for the best. In Voltaire's opinion, Leibniz and other optimists avoided the question of why evil exists in a world made by a just and all-powerful creator.

German philosopher Gottfried Leibniz. The central view of this philosophy is that everything happens for the best. Voltaire writes:

> Leibniz does not tell me by what invisible twists an eternal disorder, a chaos of

misfortunes, mingles real sorrows with our vain pleasures in the best arranged of possible universes, nor why the innocent and the guilty suffer alike this inevitable evil.

For Voltaire, it was absolutely impossible that the deaths of 90,000 innocent people could be for the best under any circumstances. "What! would the entire universe have been worse without this hellish abyss, without swallowing up Lisbon?" he asks.

"Poem on the Lisbon Disaster" was Voltaire's last published poem of any significance and one of his most important. The ideas Voltaire expressed within its lines dictated the course of the rest of his life. After its completion and his move to Ferney in 1758, Voltaire earnestly began his career as a public crusader against unjust convictions and punishments based upon intolerance.

INTERPRETING HISTORY, UNDERSTANDING SCIENCE

CHAPTER 5

Voltaire had always had an interest in history, and his passion for recording and interpreting historical events fully awakened as he composed "La Henriade." His use of historical events in his writings continued throughout his career. He made light of Joan of Arc's exploits in "La Pucelle" and captured the grief of the world in the aftermath of a historic natural disaster in "Poem on the Lisbon Disaster."

Voltaire tried to make every point as easy to grasp as possible. His histories, poems, stories, and even his scientific and philosophical writings read with refreshing clarity. Voltaire used this clarity in his historical writings to show every aspect of an event. He expanded on the work of the historian Charles-Louis Montesquieu, who pioneered a scientific method of examining history. Prior to Montesquieu, most histories were little more than a chronological list of events. Voltaire followed in Montesquieu's footsteps by considering every aspect of history. He used economics, religion, the arts, politics, and many

Charles-Louis Montesquieu was another giant of the Enlightenment. He advocated the theory of the separation of powers in his book *The Spirit of the Laws* (De L'esprit des Lois, 1748).

other facets of events being described in order to present his readers with an idea of how and why each event took place.

Many histories written at this time reflected religious orthodoxy to the detriment of the historical narrative. They essentially stated that the events described amount to little more than an irrelevant, predetermined moment between Creation and Armageddon. Voltaire set out to smash this method. He wrote to show that historical events and

circumstances were interrelated and were all important, and that their consequences carried through
the ages. In his scientific work, he used the same
clarity to explain Isaac Newton's theories to a disbe-
lieving and superstitious public.

HISTORY OF CHARLES XII

During Voltaire's exile in England, he met a Swedish
man named Fabrice. Fabrice was an old soldier who
had been a close companion to Swedish king Charles
XII. Fabrice began telling Voltaire about Charles, a
conquering ruler who had made Sweden the most
powerful nation in northern Europe during the early
eighteenth century.

Voltaire found the narrative fascinating and
took notes as Fabrice talked. He began writing *The
History of Charles XII (Histoire de Charles XII)* while
in England, though he did not have it published until

Charles XII was king of Sweden between 1697 and 1718.
Considered one of the greatest soldiers of all time, he led the
country in a series of wars that briefly made Sweden the most
powerful country in northern Europe around the turn of the eighteenth century. His reign ended when he was killed on the
battlefield in Norway. Voltaire used this portrait of the king as an
illustration in the first publication of *The History of Charles XII*.

1731. It was Voltaire's first historical work. His topic was a shrewd choice for a beginning historian. Voltaire knew that he was not experienced enough to write about a universal subject, and he did not yet have the prestige to write on French history.

The History of Charles XII examines the king's love of warfare and expansion. Voltaire describes the events of Charles XII's life and analyzes his policies as a king. He ultimately concludes that the king's rapid expansion of Sweden only brought sorrow and desolation to his own country and to Europe. He criticizes monarchy in general, noting that the only kings who deserve to have their stories told are those who have brought about great changes or who acted for the good of humanity. He writes:

> During the time that Christian princes have tried to deceive one another, and make war or conclude alliances, thousands of treaties have been signed and as many battles have been fought; fine and infamous actions are innumerable . . . Only those kings remain who have produced great changes, or those who, having been described by some great writer, emerge from the crowd, like the portraits of obscure men painted by great masters.

The end result was a compelling biography that read like a novel.

THE CENTURY OF LOUIS XIV

Voltaire began *The Century of Louis XIV* in 1732, shortly after publishing *The History of Charles XII*. The project took him almost twenty years to complete. Voltaire had to be tremendously careful with this work, since it dealt with the history of his own country. He did not want to risk offending the royal family.

The Century of Louis XIV clearly presents Voltaire's view that Louis XIV was a great king. Voltaire felt that Louis XIV deserved to be remembered not because of his wars and conquests, but for his earlier domestic policies. He praised the king's support for the arts and sciences, and noted that he had attracted many intelligent people to France with this sponsorship. Voltaire did not overlook Louis XIV's shortcomings as a ruler. He pointed out that the king's later devotion to the Catholic Church resulted in the persecution of Protestants and that his wars and lifestyle bankrupted France.

Voltaire intended for the book to be read as a tribute to the greatness of France, particularly French arts. He hoped it would encourage Louis XV to follow his predecessor's example and give generously to writers and artists. Ironically, he completed the work while living at the court of King Frederick II of Prussia, another ruler who liked to be considered a great patron of the arts. The book was finally printed in 1751 after years of polishing. Voltaire's labor paid off, and he managed to present a complex historical profile in an insightful and graceful way. The book remained one of his personal favorites.

HISTORY OF THE RUSSIAN EMPIRE UNDER PETER THE GREAT

Voltaire's next great historical subject came to him as a request from Empress Elizabeth of Russia, who invited him to write a history of Peter the Great. Voltaire accepted the assignment and began writing in 1757.

Voltaire gathered information for the biography by cultivating a vast network of Russian correspondents. His primary difficulty was in gleaning the truth from a vast quantity of letters, many from people who wished to glorify Peter the Great. "The Russians ought certainly to regard Peter as the greatest of men. From the Baltic Sea to the frontiers of China, he was a hero. But ought he to be a hero to ourselves?" wrote Voltaire in the biography. He fully intended to write the whole truth, not merely a memorial to a great man.

Voltaire finished the *History of the Russian Empire under Peter the Great (Histoire de l'Empire de Russie sous Pierre le Grand)* in 1765. The biography covered the Russian ruler's life and his efforts to modernize his nation, including his success at bringing religious authorities under control without causing a revolt. The biography is a flattering portrait of a self-educated man who made Russia economically competitive with the French and English empires.

SCIENCE AT CIREY

Voltaire had always been interested in history, but it wasn't until his exile to England that he became fascinated with science. He first wrote on scientific discoveries in several essays about the English physicist Isaac Newton's research in *Philosophical Letters*, published in 1734. His interest in scientific inquiry was rekindled by Emilie du Châtelet, an active member of France's scientific community. They set up a grand laboratory at Cirey where they could carry out experiments. Voltaire was determined to use his rationalist thinking to make scientific discoveries. They investigated the nature of optics, mechanics,

THE WORKS OF EMILIE DU CHÂTELET

Emilie du Châtelet was a very accomplished scientist during a time when few women were taken seriously as intellectuals. Along with helping Voltaire write *Elements of the Philosophy of Newton*, she also published a number of works on her own. Her most famous work is *Institutions of Physics (Institutions de Physique)*, published in 1740. This scholarly explanation of the principles of physics also speculated on the nature of God. After her death, Voltaire saw to it that her groundbreaking French translation of Newton's *Principia* was published.

This seated portrait of Emilie du Châtelet by Maurice Quentin de la Tour captures her as a serious scholar. Among her most notable works was a translation of Newton's Principia Mathematica *(Mathematical Principles).*

and with help from the scientist Samuel König, electricity. In 1737, the French Academy of Sciences ran a contest asking entrants to explain the nature of fire, then a little-understood phenomena. Both Voltaire and du Châtelet entered. They tied for honorable mention.

There were very few professional scientists during the eighteenth century. Many advances in scientific thought were made by amateurs who were curious about how the world works. French science at that time was dominated by the theories of René Descartes, a philosopher and mathematician who had advanced a number of scientific theories that failed under close examination by Newton.

Voltaire was aware that his scientific thinking was somewhat rudimentary. He decided that he could serve science best by explaining the theories of others. He largely focused his energies on understanding Newton's theories and experiments. Though Newton's ideas were well-known in England, few had heard of him in France. Voltaire wished to correct this oversight and balance out what he saw as France's faulty science. In 1738, he published his most important scientific work, *Elements of the Philosophy of Newton*.

Voltaire succeeded in making Newton's theories understandable and interesting to nonscientists. He

This is the frontispiece of Voltaire's *Elements of the Philosophy of Newton*. The illustration depicts the scientist working at a desk surrounded by books, a globe, and various mathematical and scientific tools, with the light of knowledge shining upon him. The theories and experiments of scientists helped to shatter religious explanations of the world, which gave philosophers like Voltaire ammunition to challenge Europe's religious and political authorities.

was the first to tell the famous—though untrue—story of the apple falling from the tree and hitting Newton on the head, inspiring the scientist to consider the force of gravity. Such explanations made science accessible to ordinary people. His work on Newton was particularly worthwhile because no other writer had sought to clearly explain science to a general audience.

Voltaire himself had a hard time understanding some of Newton's theories and mathematical equations. In fact, du Châtelet probably wrote the two chapters explaining Newton's mathematics. His own struggles with the science made his success with the work all the more astonishing to his contemporaries. While he continued to follow scientific discoveries or defend Newton's ideas, *Elements of the Philosophy of Newton* remains his most significant contribution to science.

THE CRUSADING PHILOSOPHER

During his lifetime, Voltaire was almost as famous for his philosophy as he was for his dramas and poetry. He was referred to as a *philosophe*, a word used to describe people such as himself, Rousseau, and Diderot, who pursued a wide variety of intellectual subjects. They focused on using their knowledge and reason for the betterment of humanity rather than on abstract thought. Many modern critics do not consider Voltaire an original philosopher because he never actually developed a philosophical system of beliefs. Instead, he either echoed the thoughts of others or pointed his readers toward more original thinkers.

Voltaire's philosophical works advocate tolerance, justice, and basic human rights. They attack established institutions that he believed stood in the way of these ideas.

Voltaire intended for his writings to educate the public and inspire social change. Some works pointed out the flaws of his own nation by praising another. Other works destroyed enemies through ridicule. Most concentrated on the subject of religious tolerance. All employ his trademark clarity of expression. Ultimately, his most important philosophical works helped awaken public opinion against injustice in the years leading up to the French Revolution.

PHILOSOPHICAL LETTERS

Philosophical Letters was Voltaire's first major philosophical work. He began working on it during his exile in England. The book was first printed there in English under the title *Letters Concerning the English Nation* in 1733. It consists of a series of essays in which he praises English society.

In its pages, Voltaire discusses all that he learned about the English during his stay. He presents a wide range of topics, including government, trade, and medicine. Voltaire speaks highly of England's religious tolerance. He devotes space to English poets, such as John Dryden, his friend Alexander Pope, and William Shakespeare. Voltaire incorporates discussions of English philosophers,

Sir Isaac Newton (1643–1727) is widely referred to as the father of modern science because of the significant contributions he made to the understanding of motion, gravity, and light. A mathematician, as well as a scientist, he invented calculus. He also produced influential writings on philosophy and history.

notably John Locke's empiricism and his belief that people have a divine right to freedom. He also writes about Sir Francis Bacon, one of the pioneers of modern scientific thought, and on the works and theories of Sir Isaac Newton.

Philosophical Letters demonstrated Voltaire's ability to investigate many different subjects and discuss them intelligently. He also proved adept at subtly criticizing his own country. His praise for England can be read as a condemnation of France. France was the opposite of England in many respects. Only one faith, Catholicism, was permitted. The French economy was in ruins while the poor paid all the taxes, whereas England grew rich from the Industrial Revolution. France's science was primitive in comparison to England's. England's tolerant government granted philosophers latitude in criticizing society, while France persecuted those who spoke against the church or the Crown. Voltaire wrote:

> If one religion only were allowed in England [as in France], the government would very possibly become arbitrary; if there were but two, the people [would] cut one another's throats; but as there are such a multitude, they all live happy and in peace.

This unattributed engraving portrays French peasant life in the seventeenth and eighteenth centuries. The lives of those in France's lower class were characterized by poverty, difficult agricultural or other manual labor, and a crushing tax burden. The vast majority of the peasants lived at or below the subsistence level, meaning that they earned just enough to feed their families.

He published *Philosophical Letters* in France in 1734. The book was banned, confirming many of Voltaire's criticisms.

TREATISE ON METAPHYSICS

Treatise on Metaphysics (Traité de Métaphysique) may be Voltaire's most truly philosophical work. In it, he attempts to answer the questions of whether God exists and, if so, what would be God's relationship to humanity. Voltaire makes relatively few mentions of God in most of his writing, despite his battles with the Catholic Church. His constant mockery of the church and of organized religion in general led many of his enemies to claim that he was an atheist.

Voltaire had briefly criticized atheism in *Philosophical Letters*, but that work revealed little of his own religious beliefs. Voltaire concludes in *Treatise on Metaphysics* that the belief in God is essentially a philosophical convenience. He dismisses efforts to scientifically prove God's existence yet casts aside efforts to disprove it. Ultimately, he decides that spirituality should be separated from the trappings of organized religion and that God should be accepted as infinite and unknowable. "It is just as absurd to say of God in this connexion that God is just or unjust as to say that God is blue or square," wrote Voltaire. He understood that this was a highly inflammatory statement to make, one that could easily get him killed by the powerful church. Though he wrote *Treatise on Metaphysics* in 1734, he never had it published during his lifetime.

ESSAY ON MANNERS

Voltaire's seven-volume *Essay on Manners (Essai sur le Moeurs)* could almost be described as a history.

Published in 1756, it is the earliest attempt by any French author to write a universal story of civilization's development. He devotes chapters to China, India, Persia, Arabic culture, and Jewish society. These discussions, like his writing about England, are used to criticize Europe, and France in particular. In his preface, Voltaire describes this work as an attempt to give an account of the nations "who live on the earth and desolate it." Voltaire remains true to his goal and tells as much of the history of these nations as contemporary knowledge allowed.

After setting the stage by describing the history, religion, and philosophy of these nations, Voltaire turns the narrative in a more philosophical direction. He begins discussing the origins and growth of Christianity. Compared with other philosophies and religions, Voltaire argues, Christianity survived and succeeded in spite of its religious content. He concludes sarcastically that Christianity must be divine in some sense because seventeen centuries of ineptitude and rascality by religious leaders had not destroyed it. Yet he praises the Catholic Church for awarding high offices based on merit, rather than social standing. From there, Voltaire moves to a general history of Europe in which he condemns historical instances of injustice and fanaticism while praising the development of the arts and learning.

PHILOSOPHICAL DICTIONARY

In 1764, Voltaire compiled all of the articles he had written for Diderot's *Encyclopedia* into a single volume called *Philosophical Dictionary*. He wrote articles about everything ranging from China to Moses, fanaticism to dreams, beauty to prejudices. The bulk of the content covers religious or philosophical topics. He takes a scientific approach to these subjects, establishing the causes and circumstances of events and phenomena.

Voltaire's technique is particularly critical of biblical topics. During his lifetime, everything in the Bible was taken as fact. Voltaire dared to interpret biblical events, putting them into perspective with other beliefs and historical occurrences. Today, such interpretations are common largely because of Voltaire's groundbreaking *Philosophical Dictionary*.

VOLTAIRE'S *CONTE PHILOSOPHIQUES*

Voltaire began writing fiction fairly late in life. He did not publish his first fictional work until 1747, when he had the story *Memnon* printed. In an almost offhanded manner, Voltaire had created a form of literature known as the *conte philosophique* (philosophical tale). This type of short fiction combined

This painting depicts the first reading of Voltaire's play *The Orphan of China* at a salon in the 1750s. Women played a major role in the salon movement. Although few women participated in the discussions, their roles as organizers and hostesses of these gatherings facilitated the crucial networking between scientists, philosophers, musicians, artists, and, sometimes, even royalty that was crucial to the Enlightenment.

storytelling techniques with the thoughtful substance of an essay. It was intended to instruct and amuse the reader at the same time. Most of these works are narrated by a wise, objective commentator. Voltaire wrote twenty-five of these stories. Today, the conte philosophiques are his best-known writings.

Voltaire began writing *Memnon* as a means of entertaining his hosts while staying with some friends in the countryside. *Memnon* later became famous under the title *Zadig*. It tells the story of a philosopher who is seeking happiness but is forced to endure persecutions at the hands of cruel, petty, and stupid men. Though the story asserts humanity's smallness against the rest of the universe, the hero does find happiness at the end.

Micromégas, published in 1752, features a being from the star Sirius who journeys to Saturn. He and a being from Saturn then travel to Earth on a scientific mission. They tower over the humans they meet, referring to these people as "insignificant atoms puffed up with an almost infinite pride." They question these "atoms" about their world and their souls, but none of the humans can give a satisfactory answer. The story illustrates the uselessness of trying to explain the complexities of the world through science and philosophy.

The Story of a Good Brahmin (*L' histoire d'un Bon Brahmin*, 1761) describes a traveler's meeting with an ancient Brahmin, an Indian wise man. They discuss the unhappiness in their lives and decide that only the ignorant can be completely content. The traveler ultimately decides that reason is more valuable than happiness. *The White Bull* (*Le Taureau Blanc*, 1774) discusses the fates of the animals represented in the Bible, such as the whale that swallowed Jonah and the serpent that tempted Eve.

VOLTAIRE'S WORDS AND LETTERS

By the end of his long life, Voltaire had published over 10 million words, an amazing figure. If all of those words were printed together, they would fill fifteen Bibles! Voltaire also composed letters constantly, right up to the day he died. He wrote to many famous people, including other writers such as Diderot and the English historian Edward Gibbon. He also corresponded with politicians such as Thomas Jefferson, Benjamin Franklin, and Russia's Catherine the Great. The bulk

of his letters went to close friends, admirers, and people seeking his help. He even wrote to his enemies, insulting Jean-Jacques Rousseau and others through the mail. Today, about 20,000 of his letters have been discovered, and more likely await discovery.

French artist Eugene Deveria imagines a meeting between Voltaire and Benjamin Franklin in this 1826 painting. Voltaire is shown engaging Franklin's grandson as he welcomes the American diplomat.

The story gently mocks humanity's certainty that the world was created for people rather than for animals.

CANDIDE

Without question, *Candide* is Voltaire's master-piece. He began writing the story soon after hearing of the Lisbon earthquake and used it to deflate the philosophy of optimism. Voltaire uses *Candide* to criticize the view that a benign God ensures that all will be for the best in this best of all possible worlds. Instead, he strives to teach his readers that the best way to improve the world is through productive work benefiting others.

The title character is a young man who is con-stantly falling victim to disasters. Candide begins his adventures by getting driven out of the castle where he lived for romancing the baron's daughter. He leaves as a youth full of innocent optimism, convinced that everything happens for the best. He allows fate to take him where it will, rather than take responsibility for his life by making choices. This optimism opens him up to an unimaginable series of disasters. Many of his troubles are brought about by dogmatic religious lead-ers and irrational philosophers.

Candide's traveling companion is Dr. Pangloss, a devoted optimist and follower of the philosopher

Le Baron....voyant cette cauſe & cet effet, chaſſa Candide
du Château à grands coups de pied dans le derriere ;

Candide Chap. 1.er

Candide is shown being driven from the baron's castle in this illustration from an early publication of the philosophical tale. The caption reads, "The baron . . . seeing this cause and effect, chases Candide from the house with a big kick in the rear end."

Leibniz. Candide witnesses the Lisbon earthquake, receives a flogging, and barely escapes from a utopian paradise that people are not allowed to leave. All the while, Pangloss's declaration that it all happens for the best in this best of all possible worlds keeps ringing in Candide's ears. As Candide experiences these hardships, he slowly comes to doubt Pangloss's philosophy. After receiving a flogging and seeing his companion hanged following the Lisbon earthquake, Candide muses:

> If this is the best of all possible worlds, what are the others like? The flogging is not so bad, I was flogged by the Bulgars. But oh my dear Pangloss, greatest of philosophers, was it necessary for me to watch you being hanged, for no reason that I can see? Oh my dear Anabaptist, best of men, was it necessary that you should be drowned in the port? Oh Miss Cunégonde, pearl of young ladies, was it necessary that you should have your belly slit open?

Candide later encounters Dr. Pangloss again and frees his friend from slavery. Candide asks the good doctor, "Now that you have been hanged, dissected, beaten to a pulp, and sentenced to the galleys, do you still think everything is for the best in this world?" Pangloss replies, "I am still of my first opinion, for after all I am a philosopher, and it would not be right for me to recant since Leibniz could not possibly be wrong, and besides pre-established harmony is the finest notion in the world . . ."

Candide and his companions eventually reach a safe haven, a large house surrounded by gardens by the Bosporus Sea. Dr. Pangloss declares that this must be the best of all possible worlds since they have landed at such a paradise.

By this time, Candide is no longer an innocent optimist. He agrees with Pangloss but cautions that "we must cultivate our garden" in case of another disaster. Voltaire's ultimate argument is that people should take active roles in their own lives, rather than let fate carry them along.

THE IMPACT OF VOLTAIRE'S WORK

Voltaire is one of history's most prolific writers. Few writers from any period have matched his knowledge, output, and clarity. Voltaire became enormously famous during his lifetime. People throughout Europe and the Americas knew and read his works. His later interest in correcting injustices won him respect, even among those who did not read.

Voltaire had many admirers, but he also had powerful enemies. His friends promoted his writings and sometimes protected him, while his enemies sought his downfall. The Catholic Church in particular wished to see him ruined.

After his death, Voltaire became an even greater figure to those who wanted to change France's social structure. For most of his life, he had

The Roman Catholic Church kept tabs on the writings of the philosophers of the Enlightenment, many of whom roundly criticized the church even though they, at times, maintained various levels of contact with religious authorities. This document, written by Voltaire, is from the Secret Archives of the Vatican, in Rome, Italy.

undermined the power of the church and of the monarchy through his writings. Just eleven years after his death, the French Revolution brought an end to the power of the Crown and greatly reduced the influence of the church.

THEATER

Voltaire began his literary career as an amusing poet, popular with many people but hardly deserving respect. The success of his production of *Oedipe* in 1718 rocketed him to fame. Many of Voltaire's later dramas received less attention and acclaim, but his renown as a playwright never diminished during his lifetime. Voltaire dominated the French theater during the eighteenth century. His sheer output of plays and their general popularity with the public were unmatched during his lifetime.

Voltaire's share of the profits from the box office during *Mérope*'s run in 1743 broke all records. The opening brought enormous crowds to the theater thanks to an early review by a Jesuit critic who called it a model of tragedy. Throughout his career, most of Voltaire's theatrical reviews were favorable.

His position among the era's actors and actresses was also unique. Theater work had a bad reputation before and during Voltaire's lifetime. Actors and actresses often worked for little money, and the Catholic Church considered their profession immoral. After making his initial fortune on *Oedipe*, Voltaire began giving his share of each play's box-office profits to the cast and crew. He also fought for the right of actors to be buried in consecrated grounds. This generosity won him the love and respect of theater workers throughout Paris.

BATTLING THE CENSORS

In France during the eighteenth century, every piece of writing had to be approved before it could be officially published. Voltaire managed to avoid censorship of his dramas throughout his life. He wrote most of them as attacks against intolerance and abuses of power, but he usually concealed his attacks by placing them within historical settings. Voltaire's devotion to clarity in his writing made it impossible for him to do the same with his poetry and history. He frequently had to publish his most controversial works under another name and deny his authorship. His wit and lucid style generally made it obvious that the writings were his, but the authorities could not prosecute him if they couldn't prove he was the author.

Voltaire first encountered trouble from the censors when he tried to have "La Henriade" published in 1723. Because it was so critical of the Catholic Church, the censors would not allow it to be printed in Paris. Voltaire eventually had the work printed outside the city and smuggled in to be sold. This practice was common during the eighteenth century. The authorities eventually relented regarding "La Henriade," but Voltaire would receive trouble from them throughout his life. Many of his works were condemned and forbidden. Remarkably, French authorities also condemned *The Century of Louis XIV*, reasoning that Voltaire's praise for

Louis XIV was simply a very clever way of criticizing Louis XV.

Despite the censors, Voltaire's works circulated widely. When *Candide* was published in 1759, Parisians were literally pulling copies out of each others' hands. Voltaire always had long lists of subscribers, people who signed up and paid for his books in advance. Copies of his works spread throughout Europe in this way and were sent along to the Americas.

VOLTAIRE'S ENEMIES

The state and religious authorities were not the only critics who battled Voltaire. Since his unfortunate run-in with the Chevalier de Rohan-Chabot, Voltaire had developed a habit of viciously defending himself against personal criticism. During his career, he was frequently attacked in journals, letters, and pamphlets. Most often, they charged that Voltaire was an amoral atheist. Voltaire usually retaliated, carrying on some of these feuds for years.

Literary critics and lesser writers jealous of Voltaire's success frequently struck out against him. The editor and critic Pierre Desfontaines went so far as to print an entire volume of accusations against

The Abbé Desfontaines emerged as Voltaire's most bitter critic during the 1730s. The ill will was a surprising development, considering that Voltaire secured a pardon for the abbé in 1725, rescuing him from being burned at the stake.

Voltaire called the *Voltairomanie* (*Voltaire's Handles*) in 1738. The *Voltairomanie* was published in retaliation to Voltaire's pamphlet *Le Préservatif* (The Defense), which had been printed earlier that year. Voltaire had written *Le Préservatif* in response to Desfontaine's constant attacks against him. The work painstakingly pointed out errors and defects in Desfontaines's writing. Nonetheless, Voltaire attempted on several occasions to heal the breach between them.

Voltaire feuded with several excellent writers as well, including the playwright and novelist Pierre Marivaux. Voltaire famously told the poet Jean-Baptiste Rousseau that Rousseau's "Ode to Posterity" would never reach its destination after Rousseau had criticized Voltaire's writing. The feud between them lasted until Rousseau's death in 1741. His quarrels with the scientist Pierre Maupertuis in Prussia ultimately led to Voltaire fleeing that country. Soon afterward, a bitter public dispute began with another Rousseau, the philosopher Jean-Jacques. Despite his antagonism toward his critics, Voltaire was a generous and loyal friend to many people.

THE REVOLUTIONARY SPIRIT

Voltaire lived through the reigns of three kings and one regent. During his lifetime, France's economy steadily declined. France became involved in the Seven Years' War in 1756, joining Sweden, Russia, and Spain in fighting Great Britain and Prussia. When the war ended in 1763, France had lost territory in North America and Europe. Voltaire and his fellow philosophers put further pressure on the palace Versailles with their writings.

Discontent grew steadily among the lower and middle classes. France became involved in the American War of Independence. Further economic disasters during the 1780s led to halfhearted reforms by Louis XVI, but it was too late. Frustrated French citizens, inspired by the success of the American Revolution, began revolting in 1789. The monarchy

VOLTAIRE VS. ROUSSEAU

Voltaire and Jean-Jacques Rousseau had been friendly correspondents for fifteen years when Charles Palissot produced a satirical play called *Les Philosophes*. The play attacked Rousseau, Diderot, and other Enlightenment thinkers but spared Voltaire. Voltaire protested and wrote to Palissot in defense of Diderot and Rousseau. However, Rousseau mistakenly assumed that Voltaire was somehow responsible for the play and wrote him

a long letter. In it, Rousseau accused Voltaire of ruining his hometown, Geneva, making it impossible for him to live there. He summed up his feelings for Voltaire with the phrase "In short, I hate you." The two were enemies from that moment until the end of their lives.

This woodcut imagines a philosophical quarrel between Voltaire and Rousseau. Despite their enmity, the two writers more often agreed than disagreed.

Louis XVI was king of France at the time of the French Revolution. The revolutionaries arrested him, tried and convicted him for treason, and later executed him and his wife, Queen Marie Antoinette. This engraving depicts the capture of the royal family in Varennes, France, after they had fled Paris.

was officially suspended in 1792. Louis XVI and his wife, Marie Antoinette, were executed the following year. A long and bloody revolutionary period followed, lasting until an ambitious military officer named Napoléon Bonaparte seized power in 1799.

VOLTAIRE TODAY

Voltaire was hailed as a hero during the early years of the revolution. In the bloody aftermath of the

Today, Voltaire's stature as a hero in French history is unquestioned. His statue stands in a crypt where he is buried in the Pantheon, a national monument in Paris, that houses France's honored dead. The inset image is of an eighteenth-century medallion in honor of the champion of the French Enlightenment.

revolution and of Napoléon's rule, which ended in 1815, the Catholic Church and conservative politicians blamed Voltaire for the revolution's violence. Grave robbers even went so far as to steal his remains and bury them in ground waste. Voltaire's reputation was gradually restored during the late nineteenth century. Today, he is once again viewed as a hero in France.

Voltaire's dramas dominated French theater during the eighteenth century and broke ground in introducing political themes to the stage. "La Henriade" remains the most celebrated poem in France's history. Voltaire dramatically influenced the way that science and history were written, though few today read his works on those subjects. Today, he is best known for his conte philosophiques. The misadventures of the hapless hero of *Candide* remain popular throughout the world. The American conductor Leonard Bernstein even turned *Candide* into a popular operetta in 1956. The humor and satire found in *Candide* and Voltaire's other fictional works continue to influence writers to experiment with absurdity and protest injustices by using humor.

Voltaire's greatest impact was in the philosophy of the Enlightenment. Throughout his lifetime, he advocated rational religions free of corrupt officials.

His activism helped bring about the practice of freedom of religion, the secularization of Europe, and the separation of church and state. His campaigns for basic human rights helped spur two revolutions, one in America and one in France, and later influenced governments all around the world to make changes regarding the treatment of their citizens.

TIMELINE

1598	King Henry IV issues the Edict of Nantes.
1685	King Louis XIV revokes the Edict of Nantes by issuing the Edict of Fontainebleau.
1694	Voltaire is born in Paris, France.
1711	Voltaire completes his education at Louis-le-grand.
1715	Louis XIV dies.
1717	Voltaire spends eleven months imprisoned in the Bastille.
1718	Voltaire's first play, *Oedipe*, premieres in Paris to wide acclaim.
1726	The Chevalier de Rohan-Chabot has Voltaire imprisoned and exiled to England.
1729	Voltaire returns to Paris.
1730	The play *Brutus* opens in Paris. Voltaire publishes "La Henriade" in French.
1731	*The History of Charles XII* is printed.
1732	*Zaïre* is performed for the first time.
1733	The poem "The Temple of Taste" appears in print.
1734	Voltaire publishes *Philosophical Letters* without official permission and is forced to go into hiding at Cirey.
1736	*Elements of the Philosophy of Newton* is published. Voltaire produces *Alzire*.
1738	*Discourse on Man* appears.
1742	Voltaire produces *Mahomet*.
1743	*Mérope* premieres at Cirey.

1745	King Louis XV appoints Voltaire royal historiographer.
1749	Emilie du Châtelet dies, and Voltaire leaves Cirey.
1750	Voltaire goes to Prussia to stay with King Frederick II.
1751	The biography *The Century of Louis XIV* is published.
1753	Voltaire sneaks out of Prussia after angering Frederick II.
1754	Voltaire moves into Les Délices, a home just outside of Geneva, Switzerland.
1755	Ninety thousand people die when an earthquake destroys the Portuguese city of Lisbon.
1758	Voltaire leaves Les Délices, moving to Ferney.
1759	*Candide* is published.
1760	Marie Corneille comes to live at Ferney.
1764	The *Philosophical Dictionary* is published.
1765	Voltaire wins acquittals for the Calas family. Diderot completes the first edition of his *Encyclopedia*.
1766	Voltaire publishes a twelve-volume edition of Corneille's works.
1774	Louis XV dies.
1778	Voltaire dies in Paris after returning to direct rehearsals of his last drama, *Irène*.

GLOSSARY

Armageddon A final battle between the forces of good and evil, said to occur at or near the end of the world.

atheist One who does not believe in God.

bureaucracy A body of appointed government officials.

censor A person who is authorized to read publications and to ban anything considered to be obscene or politically unacceptable; to ban a publication.

clergy A body of religious officials authorized to conduct services.

confessor A priest who hears confessions.

dogmatic The state of being forceful or arrogant in stating an opinion or position.

empiricism The practice of relying on observation or experimentation to make conclusions.

epic A long poem written in an elevated style and detailing the deeds of a hero.

epigram A short, witty poem or saying.

fanaticism A state of extreme enthusiasm and intense, uncritical devotion.

heretical Opposed or counter to the teachings of an established church or religion.

hierarchy A ruling body organized into ranks.

hovel A small, wretched, and often dirty house.

Industrial Revolution The widespread replacement of manual labor by machines, beginning in Great Britain during the eighteenth century.

persecution The act of causing an individual to suffer, usually on the basis of his or her beliefs.

Protestant A Christian who does not belong to either the Catholic or Orthodox Church; a Christian who broke away from the Catholic Church during the Reformation.

rationalism The practice of guiding one's actions and beliefs solely by what seems reasonable.

regent A person who rules during the childhood, absence, or incapacity of a sovereign.

salon An elegant drawing room, frequently used as a gathering point for French intellectuals during the eighteenth century.

satire Biting wit, irony, or sarcasm used to expose folly.

sect A religious denomination.

state sovereignty The power to control a nation's government without interference from other nations.

theologian One who studies religious faiths, practices, or experiences.

tragedy A drama with a sorrowful or disastrous conclusion.

utopian Referring to a society established in hopes of perfecting human interactions.

FOR MORE INFORMATION

The British Humanist Association
1 Gower Street
London, England
WC1E 6HD
020 7079 3580
Web site: http://www.humanism.org.uk

Château de Cirey—Residence
  of Voltaire
52110 Cirey-sur-Blaise
Haute-Marne, France
e-mail: janebirk@visitvoltaire.com
Web site: http://www.visitvoltaire.com

Voltaire Foundation
University of Oxford
99 Banbury Road
Oxford, England
OX2 6JX
00 44 1865 284600
e-mail: email@voltaire.ox.ac.uk
Web site: http://www.voltaire.ox.ac.uk

The Voltaire Society of America
666 Third Avenue, 27th Floor
New York, NY 10017
e-mail: iversonj@missouri.edu
Web site: http://humanities.uchicago.
  edu/homes/VSA

WEB SITES

Due to the changing nature of Internet links, The Rosen Publishing Group, Inc., has developed an online list of Web sites related to the subject of this book. This site is updated regularly. Please use this link to access the list:

http://www.rosenlinks.com/phen/volt

FOR FURTHER READING

Cooke, Timothy, ed. *The Age of the Enlightenment* (History of the Modern World), Vol. 4. New York, NY: Marshall Cavendish, 1999.

Dunn, John M. *The Enlightenment.* San Diego, CA: Greenhaven Press, 1999.

Nardo, Don, ed. *The French Revolution.* San Diego, CA: Greenhaven Press, 1999.

Ozmon, Howard. *Twelve Great Western Philosophers.* Fayetteville, GA: Oddo Publishing, 1968.

Voltaire. *Candide.* New York, NY: Bantam Books, 1988.

BIBLIOGRAPHY

Besterman, Theodore. *Voltaire*. New York, NY: Harcourt, Brace & World, Inc., 1969.

Brians, Paul. "Voltaire: *A Treatise on Toleration*." 1998. Retrieved February 3, 2005 (http://www.wsu.edu:8080/~wldciv/world_civ_reader/world_civ_reader_2/voltaire.html).

Brooks, Richard, ed. and trans. *The Selected Letters of Voltaire*. New York, NY: New York University Press, 1973.

Durant, Will, and Ariel Durant. *The Age of Voltaire* (The Story of Civilization). New York, NY: Simon and Schuster, 1965.

Edwards, Paul, ed. *Voltaire: Selections*. New York, NY: Macmillan Publishing Company, 1989.

Gay, Peter. *The Enlightenment: The Science of Freedom*. New York, NY: W. W. Norton and Company, 1969.

Hearsey, John. *Voltaire*. New York, NY: Barnes & Noble Books, 1976.

Mason, Haydn. *Voltaire: A Biography*. Baltimore, MD: Johns Hopkins University Press, 1981.

Tallentyre, S. G., trans. *Voltaire in His Letters, Being a Selection from His Correspondence.* New York, NY: G. P. Putnam's Sons, 1919.

Thaddeus, Victor. *Voltaire, Genius of Mockery.* New York, NY: Brentano's Publishers, 1928.

Voltaire. *Candide and Other Writings.* Haskell M. Block, ed. New York, NY: The Modern Library, 1956.

Voltaire. *Candide, or Optimism: A Fresh Translation, Backgrounds, Criticism.* New York, NY: W. W. Norton & Company, 1991.

INDEX

About the Author

Jason Porterfield is a writer and researcher who lives in Chicago, Illinois. He has written many books for young adults on a variety of subjects. He came to this project with an enthusiasm spurred by his long-held fascination with Voltaire's writings.

Credits

Cover Snark/Art Resource, NY; Cover (inset), pp. 1, 41, 96 (inset) Réunion des Musées Nationaux/Art Resource, NY; p. 6 Map p. 545 from CIVILIZATION PAST & PRESENT, 10th ed. by Palmira Brummett et al. Copyright © 2003 by Addison-Wesley Educational Publishers, Inc. Reprinted by permission of Pearson Education, Inc.; pp. 8, 14, 38, 40 © Getty Images; p. 9 © Leonard de Selva/Corbis; pp. 12, 80 Erich Lessing/Art Resource, NY; pp. 18, 22, 35, 57, 74 © Bettmann/Corbis; p. 24 © Time Life Pictures/Getty Images; pp. 27, 32, 50, 63, 70, 92, 94 © Lebrecht Music & Arts Photo Library; p. 28 © Gianni Dagli Orti/Corbis; p. 31 Philip Mould, Historical Portraits Ltd, London, UK/Bridgeman Art Library; pp. 45, 53, 84 © Roger-Viollet/Getty Images; p. 48 © Archivo Iconografico, S.A./Corbis; p. 61 Chateau de Versailles, France/Giraudon/Bridgeman Art Library; p. 68 Private Collection/Bridgeman Art Library; p. 76 Mary Evans Picture Library; p. 82 The Art Archive/Musée Saint Denis Reims/Dagli Orti; p. 88 © Vittoriano Rastelli/Corbis; p. 95 The Art Archive/Marc Charmet; p. 96 © Robert Holmes/Corbis

Designer: Evelyn Horovicz
Editor: Wayne Anderson
Photo Researcher: Rebecca Anguin-Cohen